Belgium To America

A De Bock Family History

CYNTHIA MARIE DE BOCK

Mount Prospect, Illinois USA

All names and identifying details of living persons have been omitted from this family history for the protection of their privacy.

Copyright © 2013 by Cynthia Marie De Bock
Edited by Douglas Van Houten

ISBN: 978-0-615-93767-0

To Rob, Mike (1958-2004), Lizz, JoAnn, Phil, Mary and Katie.

I Love You. I Bless You. I Ask God to Bless You
and to Guide You to Your Highest Good.

CONTENTS

ACKNOWLEDGMENTS

After 30 or so years of researching my family history, I feel like this book is mine. It's not really all mine though; there are many people without whose help, this research would never have happened at all.

There are so many libraries and archivists all over the world that have had a hand in this work, I could never thank them all. Instead, I offer only a sample of the kind souls that have assisted me over the years.

First of all, a huge thank you to Georges Picavet, originally from Verrebroek, who indexed that town and gave me names of ancestors all the way back to 1576. Our De Bock line goes back only to 1736 so far. I am also grateful to Georges for visiting me in the US and kindly translating a few documents and giving me information about how things were done in Belgium in the 19th century.

Years ago, a friend bought me a vase at a yard sale for 50 cents or so. The friend got it for me because it was from Belgium. On his visit to my home, Georges Picavet was kind enough to tell me that my ugly Belgian vase from the Bochf Company may be worth something. Of course, I still have it.

I am grateful to my grandfather's sister, rest in peace, from whom I got a lot of family information. My Great-Aunt Rachel spent a couple of days with me and showed me the items she had about her family and her brother's family. She was not at all short of opinions either. She pronounced her own name Rachelle not Rachel, and passed away in 1998. I wish that I'd been given more time with her. I didn't know she even existed until I was an adult.

Many thanks to the **Aarchichief du Brugges,** which I was fortunate enough to visit in January of 2013. The archivists there, even though they were closing for lunch, couldn't have been kinder or more professional. They took extra time with me to help me understand the population records of Assebroek at the turn of the 19th century and they retrieved a marriage record for me from Oostkamp. They and many other Belgian archivists helped me over the years, and I will never know their names. God Bless them all.

Last and most importantly, thanks to the Family History Library of The Church of Jesus Christ of Latter Day Saints in Salt Lake City, the Family History Centers, and FamilySearch.org. I wouldn't have gotten any research off the ground at all if not for their mission of making available copies of original microfilmed vital and other records from all over the world. God Bless them, too!

INTRODUCTION

September 8, 1982 was my 26th birthday and at the time, I was somewhat estranged from my family. I found myself wondering where I came from and if perhaps the earlier generations of my family had it more together than my parents' generation; thereby, giving me more hope for my future. My father's birthday was coming up and because I hadn't seen him in a few years, I was thinking about him and wondered where – and even if – he had been baptized. I knew he had been born in Chicago, but that's all I knew. I wondered how hard it would be to find out.

My parents had been married in the church where I had been baptized, Immaculate Conception - North Park, so I thought that would be a good place to start. They searched for Dad in their baptismal records and they could say for certain that he wasn't baptized there. As long as I had them on the phone, I asked them to send me a copy of my parents' marriage record.

I knew where mom was baptized, Saint Michael's on Cleveland Street, and since they once lived in the same neighborhood, I called that church. They didn't have Dad's baptismal record either. But again, since I had them on the phone, I asked them to send Mom's baptismal record.

Then, I called the church where my older brother had been baptized; Saint Mary of the Lake, and again no luck. Then it dawned on me that the church that married them would have to know if my parents were both baptized Christians. I called Immaculate Conception again and yes, from the marriage information that they had, they knew that Dad had been baptized in Saint Ita's church on Broadway. I had never heard of that church before.

I called Saint Ita's and Dad's baptismal record was on the way. It turned out to be much easier than I would have thought. I was prepared at the time to call every Catholic Church in the City of Chicago if I had to, because now I had a mission.

A week or so later, I received my Dad's baptismal certificate in the mail and it told me a lot; dates, names of his

Godparents, and even the name of the priest who baptized him. The best find though, was on the back of the certificate. The church listed there the other sacraments that he would have received over his lifetime, and space to write in the name of the Church if it was known. My Dad received the sacrament of Confirmation at Saint Thomas of Canterbury Church in Chicago.

I considered all this a goldmine and suddenly had a million more questions that I wanted answers to.

Growing up, whenever we asked a question of my mother, she'd always respond, "Go look it up." I can't remember ever getting a straight answer from her. My dad, on the other hand, would tell us anything we wanted to know and he instilled in us a love of learning. So between the two of them, I got a love of learning *and* the ability to search until I found the answer to almost anything.

This book is neither an academic pursuit nor historical treatise. If it were, I'd have failed miserably. It is, instead, a gift to my relations; especially my cousins near and far, who are also interested in our De Bock family history. I hope you enjoy it.

Cynthia Marie De Bock
December 2013, Mount Prospect, Illinois, USA

Part One

Flanders and Belgium

Road sign outside Verrebroek Belgium 2013

The science of family history also known as genealogy is about people, places and time. I'm not much for political history, so instead of writing a history of Belgium, I just want to give you a sense of where our ancestors lived. If you are interested in the political history of Belgium, please consult Wikipedia. It is, in my opinion, very thorough and easy to read.

Belgium is divided into three regions which are based on culture and language. Flanders is the northern part of Belgium. Two of its provinces are West Flanders (Waas Vlaanderen) and East Flanders (Oost Vlaanderen). West Flanders main city is Bruges, and East Flanders main city is Ghent. I had the great pleasure of visiting Bruges in early 2013 and it seems to be a city that stopped in time. A tourist destination to be sure, but with such old world charm you wouldn't believe. All the buildings are stone, brick, and wood;

and the feeling is of a medieval city, rather than a modern one. I visited there to see their records. The main archives in Flanders is one of those buildings around the square and lucky for me, I'd seen enough Belgian records to know what I was looking for, Aarchichief du Brugges. There I would find a couple of wonderful documents, fillers for holes in my story. But, I'm getting ahead of myself.

Verrebroek and Vrasene (pronounced Vrazhna), two miles apart, are both in East Flanders. Our De Bock family lines come from those two towns. Our De Bocks have lived there for at least the 200 years preceding their emigration from Belgium.

Assebroek and Oostkamp are about four and a half miles apart but are in West Flanders. Our Lambert side of the family comes from there.

In Flanders, the people and the language spoken are called Flemish. The language is almost the same as the Dutch spoken in The Netherlands.

In southern Belgium the language of the people is French. The people are called Walloons. The capital of Belgium is Brussels and its official languages are both Dutch and French. Brussels sits just north of the center of the country.

In 1800, Belgium was a kingdom with no king, a land that had been ruled by Roman Emperors, King of Netherlands, Germany, King of France, etc. for 1800 years or so. Belgium's vital records that still exist today are greatly due to the French influence, because the French were – and are – tenacious record-keepers.

Today, Belgium is a constitutional monarchy. That means that it has a king, but the king has no real power. In Belgium, the king is not called King Philippe of Belgium. Instead, unlike anywhere else, his official name is Philippe, King of the Belgians. I think it's nice that he's the King of the people and not the king of the map.

As an independent nation, Belgium was finally established on 21 July 1831. As much as I'd like to start our story there, my research goes back a bit further, so...

There are a couple of things about the research you need to know. First of all, my plan is to make this readable and understandable. By that I mean that I will insert comments where I feel they are necessary and also simplify the information by taking out as much duplication as I can.

Footnotes have been omitted for the sake of readability, and have been moved to endnotes. When I was first starting out in my quest for the history of my family, I didn't know or care much about citing my sources. I know, I don't believe it either! Getting all my genealogical citations noted is on my bucket list, but I chose not to make my family wait for that to be done. You're welcome. Please keep in mind that some of this material comes from conversations I have had with family both in Norway, Michigan, USA and especially conversations with my Great-Aunt Rachel. She showed me documentation before I knew better, so I don't have citations or original copies of it.

You may have already noticed that dates are always recorded as DD MMM YYYY, different from the MM/DD/YYYY that we generally use in America. This is how dates are recorded worldwide, except for here, and so this is also how genealogists record dates. It won't take you long to get used to it.

Belgian vital records, especially birth records record the child's name in Latin. In this narrative, I have followed in parentheses these Latin names with what we would know them as today in America, or the names that they were best known as.

It is very important to know that women getting married, if they were under a certain age (I believe 21 years), needed to get sworn permission from their parent(s). This comes up in our story at least twice. Also, it's interesting that it was not at all uncommon for people to have a child before marriage in order to be certain of fertility. One thing that makes researching female ancestors in Belgium a lot easier than in other places is the fact that married women do not take their husbands' names.

Family history research is never finished and I am happy to consider any corrections, advice, or input you may want to contribute. After reading this book, you will no doubt find errors and omissions of details you know about your family that I don't. Feel free to send all comments and complaints to me at cynthia.debock@gmail.com

The earliest generation of our De Bock line that I know of was Petrus (Peter) De Bock and Anna Lampers. All that I know about them is that they had a son named Jan (John).

Joannes Franciscus De Bock & Anna Petronella Ver Braeken

Joannes Franciscus (John Francis) De Bock, the son of Petrus (Peter) De Bock and Anna Lampers was born on 24 Sep 1736 in Vrasene, Beveren, Oost-Vlaanderen, Belgium. He married Anna Petronella Ver Braeken. Together they had one son, whom they named Victor.

Joannes Franciscus died on 4 Feb 1815 in the town where he was born. Although it is still unknown where his wife Anna was born, we do know that she died before 1802 in the same town, Vrasene, where they had lived together.

Victor De Bock & Maria Theresia De Tey

Victor De Bock, the son of Joannes Franciscus (John Francis) De Bock and Anna Petronella Ver Braeken was born on 3 Aug 1775 in Vrasene, Beveren, Oost-Vlaanderen, Belgium. In one source I found Victor's occupation listed as a day worker. He married Maria Theresia De Tey, the daughter of Petrus Joannes (Peter John) De Tey and Robertina De Pauw who was born on 14 Oct 1782 in Verrebroek, Beveren, Oost-Vlaanderen, Belgium.

Together they had four children. They were all born in their mother's town of Verrebroek.

Modeste De Bock was born on 10 Apr 1806.

Marie Sophia De Bock was born on 26 Aug 1810.

Gacobus (James) De Bock was born on 26 Apr 1813. (see further)

Modette De Bock was born on 10 Apr 1816.

As of this writing, it is not known where the girls lived, married, and died. Our De Bock line continues through Gacobus (James) De Bock.

Victor died on 27 Jan 1834 at age 58 and Maria Theresia died many years later on 3 Mar 1865 at age 82. They both died in Verrebroek.

Gacobus De Bock & Nathalie Van De Walle

Gacobus (James) De Bock was born on 26 Apr 1813 in Verrebroek, Beveren, Oost-Vlaanderen, Belgium. Gacobus' name has been written several ways (Gacobus, Jacobus, Jacques and Jaak), depending on the record. I suspect strongly that he was known as Jaak.

Gacobus married Nathalie Van De Walle, daughter of Petrus Joannes (Peter John) Van De Walle and Joanna Catharina (Jane Catherine) Cleys, on 10 Nov 1847 in Verrebroek. Nathalie was born on 22 Feb 1812 in Kieldrecht, Beveren, Oost-Vlaanderen, Belgium.

They had three children who were all born in Verrebroek.

Victor De Bock was born on 4 Aug 1849. (see further)

Seraphinus (Serafino) De Bock was born on 30 Mar 1851.

Josephus Leopoldus (Joseph Leopold) De Bock was born on 1 Sep 1853.

Gacobus died on 28 Mar 1886 in Verrebroek at age 72. It is not known for certain when or where Nathalie died, but it seems correct that she died in Verrebroek after June of 1904 after living until at least 92 years of age.

Victor De Bock & Clementina Coppens

Victor De Bock, the son of Gacobus (James) De Bock and Nathalie Van De Walle was born on 4 Aug 1849 in Verrebroek, Beveren, Oost-Vlaanderen, Belgium.

Victor married Clementina Coppens, daughter of Judocus Coppens and Virginia Gyselinck, on 3 Sep 1872 in Vrasene, Beveren, Oost-Vlaanderen, Belgium. Clementina was born on 24 Feb 1851 in Vrasene. All of their 11 children were also born in their mother's town of Vrasene:

Alfons De Bock was born on 2 Jan 1873. Nothing further is known about their firstborn.

Saraphina Leontina (Josephine) De Bock was born on 5 Dec 1873. (see further)

Maria Juliana De Bock was born on 30 Apr 1875 and died 24 Mar 1879 in Verrebroek at age 3.

Maria Fidelia De Bock was born on 1 Jul 1876 and lived till adulthood.

Leopold De Bock was born on 3 Aug 1877 and died on 22 Apr 1879 in Verrebroek at age 20 months.

Serafinus De Bock was born on 1 Mar 1879 and died on 14 Mar 1879 in Verrebroek at 2 weeks of age.

Jozef De Bock was born on 11 Apr 1880. (see further)

Anonyma De Bock was born and died on 7 Feb 1882 in Verrebroek. She lived less than one day.

Valentina Maria De Bock was born on 31 Mar 1884 and died sometime after 11 Nov 1903 in Nieuwkerken-Waas, Sint-Niklaas, Oost-Vlaanderen, Belgium. Valentina married Gustaaf Maes, who was born on 21 Aug 1880 in Nieuwkerken-Waas.

Silvie Marie De Bock was born on 6 Oct 1885 and died on 16 Mar 1886 in Verrebroek at the age of 5 months.

Edmond De Bock was born on 18 Mar 1887. (see further)

Carefully reading this list of children shows that of the 11 children born to Clementina and Victor, only 5 or possibly 6 of them reached adulthood. I personally found this very sad, but it was not so unusual for the times.

Clementina Coppens died in childbirth on 18 March 1887, at the age of 36. Their eldest daughter, Saraphina Leontina (Josephine), took care of what was left of the family as much as possible.

Victor De Bock fell into depression after the loss of his wife and seemed to drift. He died on 20 Jul 1917 in an institution called Merksplas, which was in Wortel, Hoogstraten, Antwerpen, Belgium. He was 67 years of age.

Merksplas-Wortel where Victor died was an institution where beggars, vagrants and the homeless were temporarily housed. There are three records written about him after his wife died.

An official statement in the MGA (Modern Municipality Archives of Verrebroek) (Repository: State Archives, Beveren-Waas) dated 11 Nov 1903 states:

> "Have appeared 1-Valentina Maria De Bock, servant, having resided previously at Nieuwkerken-Waas, age 19, now residing at Verrebroek, 2-Natalia Van De Walle, widow of Jaak [French: Jacques, English: James] De Bock, grandmother of #1,

age 91, residing at Verrebroek, 3-Pieter Jozef Barbieur, age 75, local policeman at Verrebroek, 4-Jozef Barbieur, age 81, shoe maker at Verrebroek, 5-Louis August Vermeiren, employed wooden shoe maker, age 56, residing at Verrebroek, ... in respect of the marriage planned by Valentina Maria De Bock before mentioned, to Gustaaf Maes, servant, born at Nieuwkerken on 21 Aug 1880, residing at Kieldrect, ... which Valentina Maria De Bock, daughter of Victor De bock, age 54, earth worker, and of Klementina [sic] Coppens, deceased in this municipality, ..., declare under oath that Victor De Bock, father of the first party, has no known residence in Belgium."

A letter dated 27 Jun 1904 from the Municipality of Verrebroek to the District Attorney at Dendermonde states:

"Maria Fidelia De Bock from Verrebroek 1 Jun 1876, day worker, residing at Verrebroek since birth, wishes to marry a young man from Beveren-Waas. She is indigent, her father left the municipality and never returns, residence unknown ... 'and we never have heard from him save when he turned up at the beggars institution at Merksplas, where he was in March latest, but the 30th of the month we received news that he had fled from there.' ... Grandmother would give her consent in the absence of her son Victor, father of Maria Fidelia."

In these first two cases the documents show that Victor could not be found to give consent when his daughters wanted to get married. It is clear that in the second document the grandmother that signed for Maria Fidelia was the same grandmother that signed for her sister Valentina Maria the previous year.

The third letter on the matter dated 21 Jul 1917:

"From: Ministry of Justice / Management of Benevolence / State Benevolent Colonies / Beggars house at Merksplas – Wortel To: the Mayor of Verrebroek. Viktoor [sic] De Bock, widower of Clementina Jacobs [sic], poor subject of your municipality, has died in the institution managed my me, on 20 Jul 1917. The funeral will take place on 23 Jul 1917. The subject was born at Verrebroek on 4 Aug 1849. He was the son of Jacob and of Nathalie Van De Walle (both deceased). His children allegedly reside in Verrebroek."

Lambert

Joannes Franciscus (Jan) Lambert &
Melania Sophia (Amelia) Aspeslagh

Joannes Franciscus (Jan) Lambert, son of Joannes (Jan) Lambert and Petronella Van Houtte, was born on 8 Oct 1826 in Oostkamp, Oostkamp, West-Vlaanderen, Belgium.

Joannes Franciscus (Jan) married Melania Sophia (Amelia) Aspeslagh, daughter of Henricus Richardus (Richard Henry) Aspeslagh and Josepha Felicita Gelahof, on 1 Aug 1857 in Assebroek, Brugge, West-Vlaanderen, Belgium. Melania Sophia was born on 18 Jan 1824 in Breedene, Breedene, West-Vlaanderen, Belgium.

They had one son: Emilius (Emil) Lambert. (see further)

Joannes Franciscus (Jan) died on 11 Oct 1911 in Oostkamp, Oostkamp, West-Vlaanderen, Belgium at age 85. It is unknown where or when Melania Sophia died.

Part Two

America

Our De Bock immigrant ancestors were Saraphina Leontina (Josephine) De Bock and Edmond DeBock. Later, Jozef De Bock and his family came but the ones who stayed were Edmond Florimond De Bock and his sister Rachel Clementina De Bock.

Saraphina Leontina (Josephine) along with her husband and children brought her brother Edmond to America. According to John De Clark's petition for naturalization, they emigrated from Antwerp, Belgium on or about the 1st day of September 1900 and arrived at the port of New York, NY in the United States on the S.S. Kensington. They settled in Norway, Dickenson, Michigan, USA because there was work in the iron mountain near Norway and a large Belgian population was in the process of making their homes there. Still today there is an area in Norway, Michigan called Belgium Town. John and his family became citizens of the US on 11 Oct 1909.

Edmond, Rachel and their mother came to New York on the S.S. Lapland arriving on 19 Feb 1920.

Our Lambert immigrant ancestors were Emil Lambert and his wife Zenobia Marie De Coussemacker. They also came through New York City. Their date of arrival was 16 Nov 1901 and they traveled on the S.S. Etruria from Liverpool, England. Their last place of residence had been Antwerp, Belgium. They lived in New Jersey for a time, then in New York, before finally settling in Chicago.

S.S. Eturia

Jan Baptist (John) De Clerck (De Clark) &
Saraphina Leontina (Josephine) De Bock

Jan Baptist (John) De Clerck (De Clark), son of Aloys Van De Clerck and Clara Van De Velde, was born on 28 Jul 1872 in Nieuwkerken-Waas, Sint-Niklaas, Oost-Vlaanderen, Belgium. It is unknown what Jan did in Belgium, but in America, he was a miner. Jan Baptist (John) married Saraphina Leontina (Josephine) De Bock in 1897 in Verrebroek. John and Josephine immigrated to Norway, Dickenson, Michigan, USA in about 1900 with the first two of their children. Because Josephine was the eldest daughter in her family and because her mother was deceased and her father gone, Jan and Josephine brought with them to America her youngest brother Edmond, about 16 at the time.

Together Jan Baptist De Clark and Josephine De Bock had six children:

Mari Ghislena (Lena) De Clark was born on 27 Oct 1897 in Nieuwkerken-Waas, Sint-Niklaas, Oost-Vlaanderen, Belgium. Lena married Joseph Van Damme who was a janitor, on 11 Aug 1917 in Norway, Dickinson, Michigan, USA. Joseph was born on 14 Mar 1893 in Vrasene, Beveren, Oost-Vlaanderen, Belgium. They had one son.

Arthur (Art) Van Damme who was born on 9 Apr 1920 in Norway, Dickinson, Michigan, USA. He became a famous Jazz accordionist and died in California on 15 Feb 2010. He is buried in All Saints Catholic Cemetery in Des Plaines, Illinois. Art was 89 years old at the time of his death and was survived by his wife, three children, six grandchildren and seven great-grandchildren.

Lena died on 3 Mar 1967 in Norway, Dickinson,

Michigan, USA at age 69, and was buried on 6 Mar 1967 in Norway Township Cemetery in Norway, Michigan. Joseph died on 7 May 1983 in Kaukauna, Outagamie, Wisconsin, USA at age 90, and was buried with Lena on 11 May 1983.

Arthur Joseph De Clark was born on 28 Feb 1899 in Nieuwkerken-Waas, Sint-Niklaas, Oost-Vlaanderen, Belgium and came to the USA with his parents. He was employed at the old Aragon mine, which closed in 1931. Arthur married Rose Craybex, daughter of Nicholas Crabex and Hortense Borggrave. Rose was born on 2 Jan 1902 in Norway, Dickinson, Michigan, USA. They had two children. Arthur Joseph had been a patient at the Pinecrest Medical Care Sanitarium in Powers, Michigan for six months before he died on 18 Jul 1942 at age 43. He was buried on 22 Jul 1942 in Norway Township Cemetery in Norway, Michigan. Rose died in Oct 1985 in Norway, Michigan at age 83, and was buried next to her husband.

Florensis (Lawrence) De Clark was born on 20 Nov 1905 in Norway, Dickinson, Michigan, USA. He had worked as a miner. Lawrence married Genevieve Paul, daughter of Charles Paul and Anna La Voie, on 28 Aug 1935 in St. Stephan Church in Loretto, Michigan. Genevieve was born on 11 Oct 1910 in Vulcan, Dickinson, Michigan, USA. Together they had two children. Lawrence died on 27 Apr 1988 at age 77 in Dickinson County Hospital in Iron Mountain, Michigan. He was buried on 30 Apr 1988 in Norway Township Cemetery in Norway, Michigan. Genevieve died on 18 May 1999 at age 93 in Florence Nursing Home in Florence, Wisconsin. Lawrence and Genevieve are buried together.

Marcella (Sally) De Clark was born on 26 May 1906 in Norway, Dickinson, Michigan, USA. She lived in Chicago from 1951 until at least 1983. Marcella (Sally) married Edmond Van Driessche, son of Aloys Van Driessche and Philomena De Pusseylr, on 25 May 1927 in Norway,

Dickinson, Michigan, USA. Edmond worked as a farmer and a janitor. They had two children. Edmond was born on 16 Oct 1900 in Gladstone, Delta, Michigan, USA and died on 11 Dec 1977 in Negaunee, Marquette, Michigan, USA at age 77, and was buried on 12 Dec 1977 in Norway Township Cemetery, in Norway, Michigan. As a guest of one of her children, I met Sally in the summer of 1998. Sally died on 2 Nov 2004 in Negaunee, Michigan at age 98, and was buried with her husband in Norway, Michigan.

Bridget Leona De Clark was born on 1 May 1910 in Norway, Dickinson, Michigan, USA. Her religion was listed in different places as Catholic and Jehovah's Witness. Bridget married Edward Palmcook on 29 Dec 1931 in Norway, Dickinson, Michigan, USA. Edward was born on 23 Jun 1909. They had five children. Bridget died on 8 Oct 2001 in Escanaba, Delta, Michigan, USA and was survived by her husband, two daughters and a son, eighteen grandchildren and sixteen great-grandchildren.

Oscar Charles (Toby) De Clark was born on 25 Nov 1911 in Norway, Dickinson, Michigan, USA. He worked as a miner and a pipefitter. Oscar married Clara Vermeulen, daughter of Frederick Leonardus Vermeulen and Cecelia Ludovica Dens, on 25 Apr 1936 in Norway, Michigan. Clara was born in 1912 in Norway, Dickinson, Michigan, USA. They had three children. Toby retired in 1962 in Norway, Michigan and died on 15 May 1983 in Marquette General Hospital in Marquette, Michigan at age 71, and was buried on 18 May 1983 in Norway Township Cemetery, Norway, Michigan. Clara died on 8 Aug 1990 in Norway, Dickinson, Michigan, USA at age 78, and was buried with her husband.

Jozef De Bock & Maria Florina Van Steendam

Jozef De Bock was born on 11 Apr 1880 in Verrebroek, Beveren, Oost-Vlaanderen, Belgium.

Jozef came to America perhaps twice before marrying Maria, probably first in 1898. The 1910 census says he was living with his sister and her family since 1908, in Norway, Michigan and he was single [*sic*]. He came to America again in 1912 but the war broke out in Europe so his wife and children were not able to join him until 1920.

Jozef married Maria Florina Van Steendam, daughter of Victor Van Steendam and Philomena Van Dongen, on 10 Sep 1904 in Vrasene, Beveren, Oost-Vlaanderen, Belgium. When they got married Jozef could not sign his name. The marriage record does not say why. Maria was born on 3 Jul 1884 in Vrasene, Beveren, Oost-Vlaanderen, Belgium. They had three children:

Edmond Flurimond De Bock born on 10 May 1905.[1] (see further)

Rachel Maria Clementina De Bock was born on 3 Aug 1906 in Vrasene, Beveren, Oost-Vlaanderen, Belgium and was baptized on 5 Aug 1906 also in Vrasene. Rachel came to America with her mother and brother in 1920 (see parents info). She was a member of the Belgium American Club. Rachel, a homemaker, married twice. She herself told me that her first marriage was to a man also named De Bock. Together they had one child. She next married Domien Stevens in Chicago, Cook, Illinois, USA. After their marriage, Domien adopted Rachel's daughter and Domien was the only father that their daughter ever knew. Domien was born on 13 May 1897 in Sint-Gillis-Wass, Sint-Gillis-Wass, Oost-Vlaanderen, Belgium and died on 16 Sep 1956 in Chicago, Cook, Illinois,

USA at age 59. Rachel died on 6 Mar 1998 in Chicago, Cook, Illinois, USA at age 91, and was buried on 13 Mar 1998 in St. Joseph Cemetery, River Grove, Illinois. At the time of her death, Rachel had five grandchildren and three great-grandchildren.

Hilda Maria De Bock was born on 28 Oct 1911 in Vrasene, Beveren, Oost-Vlaanderen, Belgium and died on 3 Dec 1911 at 1 month of age in Vrasene.

Jozef and Maria Florina returned to Belgium in 1930, because Maria did not like it here in America. Maria died on 14 Oct 1934 in Vrasene, at age 50, and was also buried there. Jozef died on 26 Dec 1954 also in Vrasene, at the age of 74. His death was just three and a half months after the birth of his first male grandchild. I was always told that the birth of my brother pleased Jozef very much as it carried on the family name of De Bock.

Edmond De Bock & Emily Brack
Edmond De Bock & Emily Van Goethem

Edmond De Bock was born on 18 Mar 1887 in Verrebroek, Beveren, Oost-Vlaanderen and came to the United States as a young man in 1900 with his eldest sister and her family (see John & Josephine De Clark). He served with the U.S. forces in France during WWI. Edmond worked as a miner with the Penn Iron Mining Company until it ceased operations in the Norway, Michigan area. Later he worked as a laborer in auto manufacturing. He was a member of the Hall-DeWinter Post of the American Legion and of St. Barbara's Church in Vulcan, Michigan.

Edmond first married Emily Francis Brack, daughter of Peter Brack and Josephine Van Couteren, on 3 May 1917 in Iron Mountain, Dickinson, Michigan, USA. The marriage ended in divorce. Emily was born on 20 Jan 1901 in Klingwas, A Chinecha, Luxembourg, Belgium. They had one daughter; Margaret.

When she was living, my distant cousin Sally in Negaunee, Michigan told me that when Edmond and Emily were divorced in 1918, child support had to be paid in one lump sum. Edmond didn't have enough money at the time, so he was jailed. Apparently he was so insistent that he wouldn't be locked up without his motorbike that they allowed him to be jailed with it.

Margaret De Bock was born on 16 Feb 1918 in Norway, Dickinson, Michigan, USA. She resided in Montana from November 1935 until her death. She first married Ed Danssaert and together they had three daughters. She next married Austin (Blacky) Neville. Together they had one daughter. Margaret died on 4 May 1999 at Aspen Meadows Retirement Community in Billings, Yellowstone, Montana, USA. According to her obituary, she was survived by nine grandchildren and nine great-grandchildren.

Edmond next married Emily Josephine Van Goethem, daughter of Edward Van Goethem and Maria Diericks, on 13 Dec 1919 in Norway, Dickinson, Michigan, USA. Emily was born on 1 Apr 1899 in Belgium and died on 8 Apr 1979 in Pinecrest Medical Care, Powers, Michigan at age 80, and was buried on 11 Apr 1979 in Norway Township Cemetery in Norway, Michigan. They had one son; Omar Emil De Bock.

Omar Emil De Bock was born on 17 Oct 1920 in Norway, Dickinson, Michigan, USA. He was killed in battle in World War II. He died on 30 Oct 1944 in Leyte, Philippines at age 24, and was buried on 5 Feb 1948 in Norway Township Cemetery in Norway, Michigan. I found the records shocking that he was first buried on Leyte and not brought home until more than 3 years later. A marker on his grave reads: WWII Michigan - PFC - CO L 184 Infantry WWII BSM-PH. An interesting story about my research of Omar... I received many photographs from my father, after his mother passed away. One of those photos was a handsome young man in uniform. I eventually identified the young man as my grandfather's cousin Omar, because the same photo was imbedded into the headstone at his grave.

Edmond died on 4 Apr 1969 in Iron Mountain, Dickinson, Michigan, USA (Dickinson County Hospital) at age 82, and was buried next to his wife and son, on 7 Apr 1969 in Norway Township Cemetery, Norway, Michigan. A marker on his grave reads: WWI Michgan - Pvt. Btry E 330 FA 85 DIV. At the time of his death, Edmund had three granddaughters through his daughter Margaret.

Lambert

Emilius (Emil) Lambert &
Zenobia (Jennie) Marie De Coussemacker

Emilius (Emil) Lambert was born on 12 Mar 1860 in Oostkamp, Oostkamp, West-Vlaanderen, Belgium. Little is known about him before 1901 when he came to America at the age of 41. He was a florist and owned a greenhouse in Chicago by 1920. He was Roman Catholic.

Emil married Zenobia Marie De Coussemacker, but truth be told, it is unknown where or when. Zenobia was 19 and Emil was 41 when they eloped and they did not marry in her home town of Assebroek as they did not receive permission from her parents. Regardless, they lived together and immigrated to America in 1901. Zenobia Marie De Coussemacker, the daughter of Carolus Ludovicus De Coussemacker and Maria Anna Traen was born on 18 Jun 1883 in Assebroek, Brugge, West-Vlaanderen, Belgium.

In America she was called Jennie, she was a homemaker and like Emil, was Roman Catholic. Together they had seven children.

John Lambert was born on 25 Feb 1903 in Patterson, New Jersey, USA and died in Florida, USA. John had reddish blond hair. John married a woman whose first name was Cora.

William Lambert was born on 22 November 1905 in Rutherford, New Jersey, USA.

George Lambert was born on 28 Jul 1907 in New Rochelle, Westchester, New York, USA. George's nickname was Yitz. He married Rosetta Siefert and together they had two children.

Walter Lambert was born on 14 Mar 1908 in Ossining, Westchester, New York, USA and died on 23 Apr 1988 in Chicago, Cook, Illinois, USA at age 79.

Alice Lambert was born on 11 Jun 1910 in Chicago, Cook, Illinois, USA. (see further)

Mary Lambert was born on 9 Jun 1912 in Chicago, Cook, Illinois, USA. Mary married Merlin Baumgartner in Chicago, Cook, Illinois, USA. They had one son: William.

Eleanor Lambert was born in 17 Mar 1915 in Chicago, Cook, Illinois, USA. It is known that she had red hair.

In 1905 and again in 1909 Emil, Jennie and their children visited home. In 1905 William was an infant and they returned to the US on the S.S. Kroonland on 10 Oct 1905. In 1909 Walter was an infant and they returned to the US on the S.S. Vaderland on 23 Nov 1909 and soon after moved to Chicago. Why they moved to Chicago is not known but it is known that the US Federal Census of 1910 lists the family as living at 1217 North Campbell Avenue, Chicago, Illinois. By 1920 they lived at 3339 Foster Avenue, Chicago, Illinois.

Zenobia (Jennie) died on 5 Feb 1920 in Chicago, Cook, Illinois, USA at age 36. The cause of her death was double pneumonia. She is buried in Mount Carmel Cemetery in Hillside, Illinois. Emil Lambert died on 15 Jan 1934 in Chicago, Cook, Illinois, USA at age 73, due to peritonitis after acute appendicitis. Emil is buried in St. Joseph Cemetery in River Grove, Illinois. I find it sad that as of this writing, both of their graves remain unmarked.

Part Three

Edmond Florimund De Bock & Alice Lambert

Edmond Flurimond De Bock was born on 10 May 1905 in Vrasene, Beveren, Oost-Vlaanderen, Belgium, and was christened Roman Catholic on 12 May 1905 also in Vrasene. Edmond came to America with his mother and sister in 1920. (see parent's info) As an adult, he worked as a marble cutter and later a janitor with the Chicago Public Schools. Edmond married Alice Lambert, daughter of Emilius (Emil) Lambert and Zenobie Marie De Coussemacker, on 14 Oct 1930 in Chicago, Cook, Illinois, USA. Alice was born on 11 Jun 1910 in Chicago, Illinois, USA[2]. She was a homemaker, and at times an office worker. She was educated at Senn High School and together Edmond and Alice had ten children, eight of whom are deceased.

Richard Emil De Bock was born on 21 Oct 1931 in Chicago, Cook, Illinois, USA. According to his baby book, Richard was born at 2:30am, at 5722 Kenmore Avenue, Chicago, Illinois, weighing ten pounds at birth. He received First Holy Communion on 17 May 1942 in Chicago. Richie died on 3 Sep 1945 in Chicago, Illinois at age 13. His death was due to drowning in Lake Michigan, and he was buried on 6 Sep 1945 in St. Joseph Cemetery in River Grove, Illinois.

Albert Edmond De Bock, my father, was born on 29 Sep 1932 in Chicago, Cook, Illinois, USA. He was christened at St. Ita Roman Catholic Church on 23 Oct 1932 in Chicago. His godmother was his Aunt, Mary Lambert and his godfather was Albert Triest, a cousin of his father. He was confirmed at St. Thomas of Canterbury Roman Catholic Church on 17 May 1942 in Chicago.[3] Al served in the Illinois National Guard from 29 Sep 1949 to 28 Sep 1955. He was a route salesman for a diaper company and later a bakery. He earned a General Education Diploma (GED) in about 1976. Albert married my mother, a living female, on 10 Oct 1953. The marriage ended in divorce on 11 Aug 1973. They had eight children, all living but one.

Michael Albert De Bock, son of Albert Edmond De Bock and a living female, was born on 11 Jun 1958 in Chicago, Cook, Illinois, USA.[4] He was christened on 22 Jun 1958 at St. Mark's Roman Catholic Church in Chicago.[5] His godfather was Donald Smith,[6] a cousin of his mother. His godmother was a close friend of the family. Michael was married twice and had four children. He worked as a mechanic[7] and often a stay-at-home dad. Michael died on 8 Jan 2004 in St. Joseph Hospital in Bloomington, Illinois[8] at age 45, and was buried on 13 Jan 2004 in Abraham Lincoln National Cemetery, in Elwood, Illinois.[9] The cause of his death was coronary artery disease.[10] Today, Michael has one grandchild.

Albert next married Flossie Myrtle Kneeves, daughter of Nathan Thomas Kneeves and Martha E. Cotting, on 11 Aug 1975 in Terre Haute, Vigo, Indiana, USA. Flossie was born on 3 Jul 1919 in West Union, Clark, Illinois, USA,[11] and died on 2 Apr 1988 in Chicago, Cook, Illinois, USA[12] at age 68. She was buried on 6 Apr 1988 in Grandview Cemetery in Terre Haute, Indiana.[13] They had no children together. Lastly, Albert married Edna Mae Santy Jennings on 16 Oct 1997 in Marion, Williamson, Illinois, USA. Edna Mae was born on 30 August 1921 in Sikeston, Missouri to Estel Santy and Stella White.

Albert was my father and it's only right that I would share a bit about who he was and what he was like. The following words are not mine; they belong to my sister Mary. She describes Dad both truthfully and kindly, and I would like the world to remember our dad through her eyes.

"My father was friendly and outgoing. He came to Southern Illinois not knowing a soul but me and my family. Two short years later, he had more friends and acquaintances than one would imagine, being so new to the area, and I am sure each of them heard at least one of his stories. And boy, could he tell some stories. He had a story, a riddle, or a joke for every occasion. I had the pleasure of watching him with my children as he sewed his fingers together with imaginary thread, just as he did when I was a child.

My father was a kind heart. He helped anyone he could, however he could. He had a neighbor, a proud young man, out of work with young children and a wife. My father employed this man to mow his grass and severely overpaid him each time. He lived alone yet made big pots of stew and such and took it next door saying he had more than he could possibly eat and asked if they would do him the favor of taking some so it wouldn't go to waste.

My father wasn't good at telling people how he felt about them or initiating hugs and kisses. He wasn't big on the 'I Love Yous' but I know that when I went over to Dad's my favorite soda would be in his refrigerator waiting for me and he would want me to stay awhile.

Yes, I now know that Dad loved coin collecting, crossword puzzles, and the Chicago Cubs. I know how he felt about life, politics, religion, and his family...and I know how he felt about me."[14]

Albert died on 30 Aug 1998 in Marion, Williamson, Illinois, USA at age 65, and was buried on 4 Sep 1998 in Maryhill Cemetery in Niles, Cook, Illinois, USA.[15] His grave is at lot 26 block 7 section 11. His last wife Edna died on 5 December 2013 in Parkway Manor Nursing Home in Marion, Illinois, at age 92. She is buried in Lake Creek Cemetery in Spillertown, Williamson, Illinois.[16]

Alice Madeline De Bock was born on 27 May 1934 in Chicago, Cook, Illinois, USA. She married Thomas Edward Walsh, son of James Joseph Walsh and Elizabeth Geary, on 29 Oct 1955 in Chicago, Cook, Illinois, USA. Thomas was born on 17 Sep 1933, and worked as a Director of Phildon Corp. Together they had eight children, all living save one. Thomas died in Oct 1985 in Chicago, Cook, Illinois, USA at age 52, and was buried in Mount Carmel Cemetery in Hillside, Illinois. Alice died on 26 Aug 2013 in Chicago, Illinois at age 79, and was buried on 30 Aug 2013 next to her husband.

Donald Anthony Walsh was born on 16 Nov 1959.[17] He had married and together they had two children. Donald died on 28 Mar 2005[18] at age 45, and his funeral mass was held at St. Ferdinand Church on 31 Mar 2005.[19] He was laid to rest in Abraham Lincoln National Cemetery in Elwood, Will, Illinois, USA. The cause of his death was pneumonia.

Marie Florence De Bock was born on 30 Jan 1936 in Chicago, Cook, Illinois, USA.[20] She was a payroll clerk. Marie married Alvin Elkin, son of Morris Elkin and Rachel Miller, on 10 Feb 1960 in Chicago. The marriage ended in divorce in 1983. They had two daughters. Alvin was born on 9 Jun 1934 in Chicago, Illinois. He worked as a cab driver and a car salesman. Marie died on 17 Jan 1997[21] at Northwest Community Hospital in Arlington Heights, Cook, Illinois, USA, at age 60, and was buried on 20 Jan 1997 in Westlawn Cemetery in Chicago, Illinois. Alvin died on 4 Nov 1998 in Park Ridge, Cook, Illinois, USA at age 64, and was buried on 6 Nov 1998 with Marie.

A living female, married John Anthony Walsh, son of James Joseph Walsh and Elizabeth Geary, on 19 Jan 1957 in Chicago, Cook, Illinois, USA. Together they had nine children; seven are living and two of whom died very young. John was born on 14 Mar 1935 in Chicago, Cook, Illinois, USA. He worked as a salesman. John died on 19 Oct 2012 in Bartlett, DuPage, Illinois, USA at age 77, and was buried on 24 Oct 2012 in St. Joseph Cemetery in River Grove, Illinois.

Florence Walsh, was born on 29 Dec 1958 in Chicago, Cook, Illinois, USA and died on 23 Nov 1959 in Chicago, Cook, Illinois, USA, at the age of 11 months.

Michelle Walsh, was born on 6 Feb 1964 in Chicago, Cook, Illinois, USA and died in May 1964 in Chicago, Cook, Illinois, USA, at the age of 3 months.

Joseph Domine De Bock was born on 6 Jan 1939 in Chicago, Cook, Illinois, USA. Joseph married Louise Miriam Waters, daughter of Paul Francis Waters and Elisabeth M. Zach. They had one son and the marriage ended in divorce. Joseph next married a living female with whom he had three children. Joseph died on 19 Apr 2000 in Duluth, Saint Louis, Minnesota, USA at age 61 and is buried in Minnesota.

Edmond Arthur De Bock was born on 9 Feb 1940 in Chicago, Cook, Illinois, USA. He worked as a Member I.B.E.W. #134. Edmond married Louise Miriam Waters, ex-wife of Joseph Domine De Bock. Louise was born on 27 Apr 1937 in Chicago, Cook, Illinois, USA.[22] Edmond and Louise had two children together, the marriage ended in divorce. Louise died on 5 Nov 2003 in Chicago, Illinois[23] at age 66, and was buried on 10 Nov 2003 in St. Joseph Cemetery in River Grove, Illinois.[24] Edmond next married a living female. She had a son whom Edmond adopted. He died on 4 Jun 1988 in Chicago, Cook, Illinois, USA at age 48. His body was cremated.

Raymond Joseph De Bock was born on 6 Sep 1941 in Chicago, Cook, Illinois, USA.[25] Raymond married Annette Carolyn Schiro on 13 Oct 1962 in Chicago, Cook, Illinois, USA. Together they had two daughters. Annette was born on 20 Jul 1943, died on 19 Mar 1996 in Chicago, Cook, Illinois, USA at age 52, and was buried on 23 Mar 1996. Raymond died on 4 Mar 1999 in Chicago, Cook, Illinois, USA[26] at age 57, and was buried on 9 Mar 1999 in Maryhill Cemetery in Niles, Illinois.[27]

Lawrence (Lorry) De Bock was born on 8 Aug 1943 in Chicago, Cook, Illinois, USA. He had twice been married and had two daughters with each of his wives. He died of heart failure on 1 Jul 1995 in Chicago, Cook, Illinois, USA at age 51, and was buried on 5 Jul 1995 in St. Joseph Cemetery in River Grove, IL.

The youngest child of Edmond Florimund De Bock & Alice Lambert, a living male, was born in Chicago, married and has two children.

Edmond Florimund De Bock died on 21 Sep 1967 in Chicago, Cook, Illinois, USA at age 62, and was buried on 25 Sep 1967 in St. Joseph Cemetery in River Grove, Illinois.[28] Alice Lambert De Bock died on 10 Jul 1992 in Chicago, Cook, Illinois, USA[29] at age 82, and was laid to rest on 13 Jul 1992 with her husband.[30]

---

[1] Funeral or mass card, Born May 10, 1905.
[2] Funeral or Mass Card, Born June 11, 1910.
[3] "Certificate of Baptism." Signed on 8 Sep 1982 by Rev. Richard J. Feller.
[4] "Certificate of Baptism." 11 June 1958.
[5] "Certificate of Baptism." 22 June 1958.
[6] "Certificate of Baptism," Donald Smith
[7] Death Certificate, usual Occupation Mechanic, Kind of business or Industry: Transportation.
[8] Death Certificate, January 8, 2004.
[9] Death Certificate, Abraham Lincoln National Cemetery.
[10] Death Certificate, Coronary Artery Disease.
[11] Funeral or Mass Card, Born July 3, 1919.
[12] Funeral or Mass Card, At Rest April 2, 1988.
[13] Funeral or Mass Card, Interment April 6, 1988.
[14] "My Father" eulogy given by Mary A De Bock 4 Sep 1998.
[15] Funeral or Mass Card, Mass of Christian Burial.
[16] Obituary, Pyle Funeral Home, printed on December 8, 2013.
[17] Funeral or Mass Card, 16 Nov 1959.
[18] Funeral or Mass Card, 28 Mar 2005.
[19] Funeral or Mass Card, 31 Mar 2005.
[20] Funeral or Mass Card, Born January 30, 1936.
[21] Funeral or Mass Card, At Rest January 17, 1997.
[22] Funeral or Mass Card, April 27, 1937.
[23] Funeral or Mass Card, November 5, 2003.
[24] Funeral or Mass Card, November 10, 2003.
[25] Funeral or Mass Card, Born September 6, 1941.
[26] Funeral or Mass Card, Died March 4, 1999.
[27] Funeral or Mass Card, Laid to Rest March 9, 1999.
[28] Funeral or Mass Card, Passed Away September 21, 1967.
[29] Funeral or Mass Card, At Rest July 10, 1992.
[30] Funeral or Mass Card, Mass of Christian Burial July 13, 1992 at 10:00AM

Part Four

Direct Ancestors of
Albert Edmond De Bock

I am including my dad's ahnentafel not only because it might help in understanding but also because it goes back much further than the De Bock line alone. True, as we go back in time, fewer details are available on each person but the names alone can give us the feeling that we've been here a long, long time and somehow we really are connected to each other. At least it does that for me. Also, all those missing names and dates and places provide me with more work to do.

1. Albert Edmond De Bock, son of Edmond Flurimond De Bock and Alice Lambert, was born on 29 Sep 1932 in Chicago, Cook, Illinois, USA, died on 30 Aug 1998 in Marion, Williamson, Illinois, USA at age 65, and was buried on 4 Sep 1998 in Niles, Cook, Illinois, USA.[1]

Parents

2. Edmond Flurimond De Bock, son of Jozef De Bock and Maria Florina Van Steendam, was born on 10 May 1905 in Vrasene, Beveren, Oost-Vlaanderen, Belgium,[2] died on 21 Sep 1967 in Chicago, Cook, Illinois, USA[3] at age 62, and was buried on 25 Sep 1967 in River Grove, Cook, Illinois, USA. Edmond married Alice Lambert on 14 Oct 1930 in Chicago, Cook, Illinois, USA.

3. Alice Lambert, daughter of Emilius (Emil) Lambert and Zenobie Marie De Coussemacker, was born on 11 Jun 1910 in Chicago, Cook, Illinois, USA,[4] died on 10 Jul 1992 in Chicago, Cook, Illinois, USA[5] at age 82, and was buried on 13 Jul 1992 in River Grove, Cook, Illinois, USA.[6]

Grandparents

4. Jozef De Bock, son of Victor De Bock and Clementina Coppens, was born on 11 Apr 1880 in Verrebroek, Beveren, Oost-Vlaanderen, Belgium and died on 26 Dec 1954 in Vrasene, Beveren, Oost-Vlaanderen, Belgium at age 74. Jozef married Maria Florina Van Steendam on 10 Sep 1904 in Vrasene, Beveren, Oost-Vlaanderen, Belgium.

5. Maria Florina Van Steendam, daughter of Victor Van Steendam and Philomena Van Dongen, was born on 3 Jul 1884 in Vrasene, Beveren, Oost-Vlaanderen, Belgium, died on 14 Oct 1934 in Vrasene, Beveren, Oost-Vlaanderen, Belgium at age 50, and was buried in Vrasene, Beveren, Oost-Vlaanderen, Belgium.

6. Emilius (Emil) Lambert, son of Joannes Franciscus (Jan) Lambert and Melania Sophia (Amelia) Aspeslagh, was born on 12 Mar 1860 in Oostkamp, Oostkamp, West-Vlaanderen, Belgium, died on 15 Jan 1934 in Chicago, Cook, Illinois, USA at age 73, and was buried in River Grove, Cook, Illinois, USA. Emilius married Zenobie Marie De Coussemacker in about 1899.

7. Zenobie Marie De Coussemacker, daughter of Carolus Ludovicus De Coussemacker and Maria Anna Traen, was born on 18 Jun 1883 in Assebroek, Brugge, West-Vlaanderen, Belgium, died on 5 Feb 1920 in Chicago, Cook, Illinois, USA at age 36, and was buried on 7 Feb 1920 in Hillside, Cook, Illinois, USA. The cause of her death was double pneumonia.

8. Victor De Bock, son of Gacobus (Jacobus)(Jacques) De Bock and Nathalie Van De Walle, was born on 4 Aug 1849 in Verrebroek, Beveren, Oost-Vlaanderen, Belgium and died on 20 Jul 1917 in Merksplas, Merksplas, Antwerpen, Belgium or Wortel, Hoogstraten, Antwerpen, Belgium at age 67. Victor married Clementina Coppens on 3 Sep 1872 in Vrasene, Beveren, Oost-Vlaanderen, Belgium.

9. Clementina Coppens, daughter of Judocus Coppens and Virginia Gyselinck, was born on 24 Feb 1851 in Vrasene, Beveren, Oost-Vlaanderen, Belgium and died on 18 Mar 1887 in Verrebroek (Fort), Beveren, Oost-Vlaanderen, Belgium at age 36.

10. Victor Van Steendam, was born about 1833 and died on 15 Sep 1893 in Vrasene, Beveren, Oost-Vlaanderen, Belgium about age 60. Victor married Philomena Van Dongen.

11. Philomena Van Dongen, daughter of Ludovicus Jacobus Van Dongen and Antonia Goeman, was born on 8 Mar 1844 in Vrasene, Beveren, Oost-Vlaanderen, Belgium and died on 2 Jan 1918 in Vrasene, Beveren, Oost-Vlaanderen, Belgium at age 73.

12. Joannes Franciscus (Jan) Lambert, son of Joannes (Jan) Lambert and Petronella Van Houtte, was born on 8 Oct 1826 in Oostkamp, Oostkamp, West-Vlaanderen, Belgium and died on 11 Oct 1911 in Oostkamp, Oostkamp, West-Vlaanderen, Belgium at age 85. Joannes married Melania Sophia (Amelia) Aspeslagh on 1 Aug 1857 in Assebroek, Brugge, West-Vlaanderen, Belgium.

13. Melania Sophia (Amelia) Aspeslagh, daughter of Henricus Richardus Aspeslagh and Josepha Felicita Gelahof, was born on 18 Jan 1824 in Breedene, Breedene, West-Vlaanderen, Belgium.

14. Carolus Ludovicus De Coussemacker, was born on 15 Apr 1852 in Oedelem, Beernem, West-Vlaanderen, Belgium. Carolus married Maria Anna Traen.

15. Maria Anna Traen, was born on 12 May 1856 in Varsenare, Jabbeke, West-Vlaanderen, Belgium and died on 29 Nov 1949 in Assebroek, Brugge, West-Vlaanderen, Belgium at age 93.

Great Great-Grandparents

16. Gacobus (Jacobus)(Jacques) De Bock, son of Victor De Bock and Maria Theresia De Tey, was born on 26 Apr 1813 in Verrebroek, Beveren, Oost-Vlaanderen, Belgium and died on 28 Mar 1886 in Verrebroek (Zwaantje), Beveren, Oost-Vlaanderen, Belgium at age 72. Gacobus married Nathalie Van De Walle on 10 Nov 1847 in Verrebroek, Beveren, Oost-Vlaanderen, Belgium.

17. Nathalie Van De Walle, daughter of Petrus Joannes Van De Walle and Joanna Catharina Cleys, was born on 22 Feb 1812 in Kieldrecht, Beveren, Oost-Vlaanderen, Belgium.

18. Judocus Coppens was born on 3 Dec 1810 in Vrasene, Beveren, Oost-Vlaanderen, Belgium. Judocus married Virginia Gyselinck.

19. Virginia Gyselinck was born on 25 Aug 1814 in Vrasene, Beveren, Oost-Vlaanderen, Belgium.

22. Ludovicus Jacobus Van Dongen married Antonia Goeman. Antonia.

23. Antonia Goeman died on 7 Dec 1845 in Vrasene, Beveren, Oost-Vlaanderen, Belgium.

24. Joannes (Jan) Lambert died in Oostkamp, Oostkamp,

West-Vlaanderen, Belgium. Joannes married Petronella Van Houtte.

25. Petronella Van Houtte.

26. Henricus Richardus Aspeslagh married Josepha Felicita Gelahof.

27. Josepha Felicita Gelahof died on 15 Mar 1848 in Breedene, Breedene, West-Vlaanderen, Belgium.

3rd Great-Grandparents

32. Victor De Bock, son of Joannes Franciscus De Bock and Anna Petronella Ver Braeken, was born on 3 Aug 1775 in Vrasene, Beveren, Oost-Vlaanderen, Belgium and died on 27 Jan 1834 in Verrebroek, Beveren, Oost-Vlaanderen, Belgium at age 58. Victor married Maria Theresia De Tey.

33. Maria Theresia De Tey, daughter of Petrus Joannes De Tey and Robertina De Pauw, was born on 14 Oct 1782 in Verrebroek, Beveren, Oost-Vlaanderen, Belgium and died on 3 Mar 1865 in Verrebroek, Beveren, Oost-Vlaanderen, Belgium at age 82.

34. Petrus Joannes Van De Walle, son of Sebastianus Van De Walle and Anna Catharina Bleyenberg, was born on 21 Mar 1790 in Kieldrecht, Beveren, Oost-Vlaanderen, Belgium and died on 27 Oct 1880 in Verrebroek (Zwaantje), Beveren, Oost-Vlaanderen, Belgium at age 90. Petrus married Joanna Catharina Cleys.

35. Joanna Catharina Cleys, daughter of Josephus Cleys and Elisabetha Theresia Ver Weirden, was born on 11 May 1789 in Verrebroek, Beveren, Oost-Vlaanderen, Belgium and died on 25 Jul 1854 in Verrebroek (Rijkstraat), Beveren, Oost-Vlaanderen, Belgium at age 65.

64. Joannes Franciscus De Bock, son of Petrus De Bock and Anna Lampers, was born on 24 Sep 1736 in Vrasene, Beveren, Oost-Vlaanderen, Belgium and died on 4 Feb 1815 in Vrasene, Beveren, Oost-Vlaanderen, Belgium at age 78. Joannes married Anna Petronella Ver Braeken.

65. Anna Petronella Ver Braeken died before 1802 in Vrasene, Beveren, Oost-Vlaanderen, Belgium.

66. Petrus Joannes De Tey, son of Petrus De Tey and Maria Anna Van Hoeck, was born on 21 Jul 1752 in Verrebroek, Beveren, Oost-Vlaanderen, Belgium and died on 2 Jan 1824 in Verrebroek, Beveren, Oost-Vlaanderen, Belgium at age 71. Petrus married Robertina De Pauw.

67. Robertina De Pauw daughter of Arnoldus De Pauw and Joanna Van Esbroeck, was born on 12 Feb 1753 in Verrebroek, Beveren, Oost-Vlaanderen, Belgium and died on 29 May 1803 in Verrebroek, Beveren, Oost-Vlaanderen, Belgium at age 50.

68. Sebastianus Van De Walle died in 1811 in Kieldrecht, Beveren, Oost-Vlaanderen, Belgium. Sebastianus married Anna Catharina Bleyenberg.

69. Anna Catharina Bleyenberg died on 28 Nov 1798 in De Klinge, Sint-Gillis-Waas, Oost-Vlaanderen, Belgium.

70. Josephus Cleys, son of Petrus Cleys and Bernardina De Caluwe, was born on 21 Aug 1759 in Verrebroek, Beveren, Oost-Vlaanderen, Belgium and died on 28 Dec 1830 in Verrebroek (Rijkstraat), Beveren, Oost-Vlaanderen, Belgium at age 71. Josephus married Elisabetha Theresia Ver Weirden.

71. Elisabetha Theresia Ver Weirden, was born about 1765 in Haasdonk, Beveren, Oost-Vlaanderen, Belgium and died

on 22 May 1790 in Verrebroek, Beveren, Oost-Vlaanderen, Belgium about age 25.

5th Great-Grandparents

128. Petrus De Bock died before 1802 in Vrasene, Beveren, Oost-Vlaanderen, Belgium. Petrus married Anna Lampers.

129. Anna Lampers died before 1802 in Vrasene, Beveren, Oost-Vlaanderen, Belgium.

132. Petrus De Tey was born about 1711 and died on 8 Oct 1781 in Verrebroek, Beveren, Oost-Vlaanderen, Belgium about age 70. Petrus married Maria Anna Van Hoeck.

133. Maria Anna Van Hoeck, daughter of Judocus Van Hoeck and Anna Van Aelst, was born on 20 Feb 1714/15 in Meerdonk, Sint-Gillis-Waas, Oost-Vlaanderen, Belgium and died on 8 Feb 1797 in Verrebroek, Beveren, Oost-Vlaanderen, Belgium at age 81.

134. Arnoldus De Pauw, son of Joannes De Pauw and Sara Claus, was born on 28 May 1714 in Verrebroek, Beveren, Oost-Vlaanderen, Belgium and died on 1 Sep 1774 in Verrebroek, Beveren, Oost-Vlaanderen, Belgium at age 60. Arnoldus married Joanna Van Esbroeck.

135. Joanna Van Esbroeck was born about 1720 and died on 15 Jun 1763 in Verrebroek, Beveren, Oost-Vlaanderen, Belgium about age 43.

140. Petrus Cleys died on 8 Aug 1783 or 7 Mar 1780 in Verrebroek, Beveren, Oost-Vlaanderen, Belgium. Petrus married Bernardina De Caluwe.

141. Bernardina De Caluwe died on 11 May 1805 in Verrebroek, Beveren, Oost-Vlaanderen, Belgium.

6th Great-Grandparents

266. Judocus Van Hoeck, son of Egidius Van Hoeck and Anna Van Leugenhage, was born on 24 Nov 1683 in Verrebroek, Beveren, Oost-Vlaanderen, Belgium and died before 19 Oct 1746. Judocus married Anna Van Aelst.

267. Anna Van Aelst, daughter of Laurentius Van Aelst and Maria Van Strydonck, was born on 23 Jan 1683/84 in Verrebroek, Beveren, Oost-Vlaanderen, Belgium and died on 24 Oct 1745 in Kieldrecht, Beveren, Oost-Vlaanderen, Belgium at age 61.

268. Joannes De Pauw, son of Eduardus De Pauw. Joannes married Sara Claus.

269. Sara Claus died before 9 Apr 1723.

7th Great-Grandparents

532. Egidius Van Hoeck, son of Egidius Van Hoeck, was born about 1653 and died on 16 Sep 1746 in Verrebroek, Beveren, Oost-Vlaanderen, Belgium about age 93. Egidius married Anna Van Leugenhage.

533. Anna Van Leugenhage, daughter of Petrus Van Leugenhaghe and Elisabeth Van Vyvere, was born about 1656 and died on 1 Oct 1734 in Verrebroek, Beveren, Oost-Vlaanderen, Belgium about age 78.

534. Laurentius Van Aelst, son of Joos Van Aelst and Margareta Van Puyenbroeck, was born on 6 Jan 1653/54 in Sint-Niklaas, Sint-Niklaas, Oost-Vlaanderen, Belgium and died on 19 Feb 1704/05 in Verrebroek, Beveren, Oost-Vlaanderen, Belgium at age 51. Laurentius married Maria Van Strydonck.

535. Maria Van Strydonck, daughter of Joannes Van Strydonck and Cornelia Cramps, was born on 1 Oct 1662 in

Vrasene, Beveren, Oost-Vlaanderen, Belgium and died on 12 Jun 1720 in Verrebroek, Beveren, Oost-Vlaanderen, Belgium at age 57.

536. Eduardus De Pauw.

8th Great-Grandparents

1064. Egidius Van Hoeck.

1066. Petrus Van Leugenhaghe, died before 18 May 1685. Petrus married Elisabeth Van Vyvere.

1067. Elisabeth Van Vyvere, daughter of Jan Van Vyvere and Katelyne Van Bogaert.

1068. Joos Van Aelst, son of Willem Van Aelst and Cornelia Potters, was born on 10 Feb 1618/19 in Belsele, Sint-Niklaas, Oost-Vlaanderen, Belgium and died on 24 Sep 1668 in Sint-Niklaas, Sint-Niklaas, Oost-Vlaanderen, Belgium at age 49. Joos married Margareta Van Puyenbroeck.

1069. Margareta Van Puyenbroeck, daughter of Laurentius Van Puyenbroeck and Elisabeth Maes, was born on 22 Oct 1623 in Sint-Niklaas, Sint-Niklaas, Oost-Vlaanderen, Belgium and died on 14 Sep 1692 in Sint-Niklaas, Sint-Niklaas, Oost-Vlaanderen, Belgium at age 68.

1070. Joannes Van Strydonck. Joannes married Cornelia Cramps.

1071. Cornelia Cramps.

9th Great-Grandparents

2134. Jan Van Vyvere. Jan married Katelyne Van Bogaert.

2135. Katelyne Van Bogaert.

2136. Willem Van Aelst was born about 1576 and died on 20 Jan 1632/33 in Belsele, Sint-Niklaas, Oost-Vlaanderen, Belgium about age 57. Willem married Cornelia Potters.

2137. Cornelia Potters died after 1633.

2138. Laurentius Van Puyenbroeck. Laurentius married Elisabeth Maes.

2139. Elisabeth Maes.

Source Citations for Ahnentafel

1. Funeral or Mass Card, Mass of Christian Burial.
2. Funeral or Mass Card, Born May 10, 1905.
3. Funeral or Mass Card, Passed Away September 21, 1967.
4. Funeral or Mass Card, Born June 10, 1910.
5. Funeral or Mass Card, At Rest July 10, 1992.
6. Funeral or Mass Card, Mass of Christian Burial July 13, 1992 at 10:00AM.

Photos

In Norway, Michigan, USA – Standing left to right- Lawrence De Clark; Joseph Van Damme (Lena's Husband); Edmond De Bock (Josephine's brother); Arthur De Clark; Marcella (Sally) De Clark Van Driessche (she didn't like this photograph so she scratched her eyes out). Sitting Lena De Clark Van Damme; Josephine De Bock DeClark; Bridget DeClark Palmcook; John DeClark; standing r front Oscar De Clark.

Belgium Town Road, Norway, Michigan, USA – Josephine De Bock and John DeClark's house. Josephine with Marcella (Sally), Lawrence and Arthur on right.

Verrebroek, Belgium. Maria Fedalia De Bock (l) and
her sister Leontine (Josephine) De Bock (r)

Norway, Michigan. Edmond De Bock (l) and his brother Jozef De Bock (r)

Edmond De Bock c. 1918

Omar De Bock c. 1942

Edmond De Bock and Emily Van Goethem on their wedding day in 1919.

Edmond's daughter Margaret De Bock as a young girl.

~Arthur VanDamme~
Boy Wonder Accordionist and Entertainer
Vaudeville Stage Sensation
FOR ENGAGEMENTS: WRITE E. PINES CAVIANI. MGR. AND TEACHER
702 NORWAY ST.   IRON MOUNTAIN, MICHIGAN   PHONE 1490W

Norway, Michigan or Chicago, Illinois c. 1924. Standing Maria Florina Van Steendam De Bock. Sitting, Lena De Clark Van Damme and her son Art Van Damme.

Maria Florina Van Steendam De Bock and her husband Jozef De Bock.

Vrasene, Belgium c. 1910 – Edmond F De Bock and his sister Rachel Clementina De Bock

Rachel De Bock Stevens and her father Jozef De Bock.

Jozef De Bock

Chicago, Illinois 1953 – (l to r) Domien Stevens, Edmond F De Bock,
Lena Van Damme, and Rachel De Bock Stevens.

Chicago, Illinois c. 1952 – Edmond F. De Bock & Alice Lambert De Bock and Family.

Belgium c. 1899 – De Coussemacker family

Passaic, New Jersey c. 1902 –
Zenobia Marie (Jennie) De Coussemacker Lambert

Chicago, Illinois c. 1922 - Emil Lambert and daughters Alice, Mary, and Eleanor.

www.ingramcontent.com/pod-product-compliance
Lightning Source LLC
Chambersburg PA
CBHW041215270326
41930CB00001B/23